KAKURE Secret's of

By: Yoshida Yuki

A NOTE FROM THE AUTHOR   4

INTRODUCTION   5

CHAPTER 1: SEASONS AND FESTIVITIES MAPPING YOUR ADVENTURE   12

1.1 A LAND DEFINED BY SEASONAL CHANGE   12
1.2 SPRING (MARCH–MAY): REBIRTH AND RENEWAL   14
1.3 SUMMER (JUNE–AUGUST): FESTIVALS AND COASTAL ADVENTURES   16
1.4 AUTUMN (SEPTEMBER–NOVEMBER): FOLIAGE AND HARVEST RITUALS   18
1.5 WINTER (DECEMBER–FEBRUARY): SNOWY LANDSCAPES AND ILLUMINATIONS   20
1.6 REGIONAL VARIATIONS WORTH NOTING   21
1.7 FESTIVALS: A DEEPER LOOK   22
1.8 SEASONAL TRAVEL STRATEGIES   23
1.9 SAMPLE SEASONAL ITINERARIES   25
1.10 CHAPTER 1 SUMMARY   27

CHAPTER 2: QUIET VILLAGES IN THE MOUNTAINS   28

2.1 DISCOVERING MOUNTAIN LIFE: A RETREAT FROM MODERNITY   28

2.2 SHIRAKAWA-GO AND GOKAYAMA: ICONS OF ALPINE HERITAGE   30

2.3 KISO VALLEY: ECHOES OF THE EDO ERA   32

2.4 BEYOND HONSHU: KYUSHU'S ALPINE RETREATS   34

2.5 THE IYA VALLEY: SHIKOKU'S HIDDEN FRONTIER   35

2.6 HANDS-ON EXPERIENCES IN MOUNTAIN HAMLETS   36

2.7 PRACTICAL TIPS FOR MOUNTAIN TRAVEL   38

2.8 SPOTLIGHT: LESSER-KNOWN ALPINE GEMS   38

2.9 CHAPTER 2 SUMMARY   39

CHAPTER 3: COASTAL ESCAPES AND HIDDEN BEACHES   40

3.1 THE DIVERSITY OF JAPAN'S COASTLINES   40

3.2 HIDDEN FISHING VILLAGES AND THEIR ALLURE   43

3.3 REMOTE BEACHES AND ISLAND ADVENTURES   46

3.4 CULTURAL GEMS ALONG THE COAST   49

3.5 TIPS FOR COASTAL EXPLORATION   51

3.6 CHAPTER 3 SUMMARY   53

CHAPTER 4: SERENITY IN GARDENS AND NATURE RESERVES   54

4.1 A BRIEF HISTORY OF JAPANESE GARDENING   54

4.2 CITY GARDENS AND HIDDEN URBAN OASES   57

4.3 NATURE RESERVES AND NATIONAL PARKS   60

4.4 FOREST BATHING AND RECONNECTING WITH NATURE   62

4.5 OFF-THE-BEATEN-PATH GARDENS AND RESERVES   64

4.6 PRACTICAL TIPS FOR GARDEN AND NATURE-RESERVE VISITS   66

4.7 CHAPTER 4 SUMMARY   68

CHAPTER 5: OFFBEAT CITIES & TOWNS WITH QUIRKY CHARM   69

5.1 WHY VENTURE OFF THE MAIN TOURIST TRAIL?   69
5.2 QUIRKY URBAN CENTERS   71
5.3 LESSER-KNOWN TOWNS WITH SURPRISING TWISTS   74
5.4 QUIRK-DRIVEN TOURISM & LOCAL PRIDE   77
5.5 THE VALUE OF OFFBEAT FESTIVALS   78
5.6 PRACTICAL TIPS FOR EXPLORING QUIRKY CITIES & TOWNS   80
5.7 CHAPTER 5 SUMMARY   82

CHAPTER 6: CULINARY SECRETS   83

6.1 BEYOND SUSHI & RAMEN   83
6.2 HIDDEN IZAKAYAS AND NIGHTLIFE SCENES   86
6.3 FAMILY-RUN EATERIES: HEART OF THE NEIGHBORHOOD   89
6.4 UNDERGROUND DINING & SECRET POP-UPS   91
6.5 SAKE, SHOCHU & CRAFT BEER   92
6.6 PRACTICAL TIPS FOR CULINARY EXPLORATIONS   95
6.7 CHAPTER 6 SUMMARY   98

CONCLUSION   98

A Note from the Author

Hello, dear reader! My name is **Yoshida Yuki**, and I am delighted that you've picked up this book. Japan is a land often characterized by its neon-lit cities, bullet trains, and bustling tourism hotspots like Tokyo and Kyoto. While these iconic destinations are undoubtedly fascinating, there is so much more waiting to be discovered beyond the well-trodden paths.

Over the years, I've had the privilege of exploring the lesser-known corners of my homeland—small villages hidden in the fog of mountain valleys, serene coastal towns nearly untouched by modern development, and secret restaurants where the day's special isn't on the menu board but whispered by the chef. In these underexplored locales, you'll find a different rhythm of life and a treasure trove of stories and experiences that connect you with Japan's rich, layered culture.

With this book, I want to share the enchanting side of Japan that is often overshadowed by more famous tourist stops. It is my hope that by peeling back the layers, we can venture together into lush forests, century-old teahouses, secluded beaches, and lively local festivals rarely mentioned on mainstream travel sites. Whether you're a first-time visitor or a seasoned traveler, you'll discover a country brimming with surprises and depth.

Introduction

Greetings, fellow wanderer! My name is **Yoshida Yuki**, and it's my pleasure to welcome you to this journey into Japan's hidden corners. We all know the iconic images of neon-lit Shibuya crossings and the timeless temples of Kyoto—but beyond these well-trodden paths lie countless other experiences that rarely make it to the headlines. From silent mountain hamlets and lesser-known coastal sanctuaries to family-run eateries and artisan enclaves, these overlooked destinations are where Japan reveals some of its most intimate stories.

Why Venture into the Unknown?

Modern tourism often spotlights the same handful of major cities and famous landmarks, but Japan's most compelling allure can be found in places you won't see plastered across social media. Perhaps it's a remote fishing village where the morning catch shapes the entire day's meals, or a tiny train station that still hand-stamps tickets—offering a nostalgic glimpse into pre-digital life. By stepping off the standard travel itinerary, you allow serendipity to guide you toward spontaneous encounters and authentic cultural exchanges.

The Beauty of Unpredictability

Hidden gems rarely present themselves on a tight schedule. One moment, you may be chatting with a stranger in a local market who offers directions to a scenic shrine tucked away in a bamboo grove; the next, you're wandering winding backstreets that reveal a decades-old sweet shop serving handmade wagashi. It's this sense of unpredictability—where each twist and turn can lead to something extraordinary—that defines off-the-beaten-path travel in Japan. Rather than racing through must-see stops, you adapt to the unhurried pulse of small towns and rustic neighborhoods.

Embracing Slower Rhythms

These lesser-explored regions ask you to slow down, encouraging deep, reflective experiences rather than superficial snapshots. You might find yourself sipping tea at an artisan's workshop, the walls lined with family heirlooms and half-finished creations, as your host explains the generational techniques behind each piece of pottery. Or perhaps you'll join in a neighborhood harvest event—a local festival celebrating the rice paddy's yield or a communal sweet potato roast over open flames. Such personal interactions provide a more profound sense of place and memory, forging a bond that transcends language barriers and fleeting tourism.

The Spirit of Omotenashi

One of the most remarkable aspects of traveling in Japan is **omotenashi**: a heartfelt hospitality rooted in anticipation of guests' needs. While megacities also practice it, omotenashi sparkles most brilliantly in quieter corners of the country, where traditions remain deeply interwoven with daily routines. An elderly innkeeper may greet you not merely as a customer, but as an honored guest—someone to be offered seasonal fruit from her backyard orchard or local sweets made according to a passed-down family recipe.

A Two-Way Exchange

Of course, hospitality is never one-sided. Simple gestures—like greeting store owners with a polite "Konnichiwa," learning a few regional dialect phrases, or observing local etiquette at shrines—can quickly bridge cultural gaps. Show genuine curiosity, and you'll likely be rewarded with stories, tips for hidden scenic spots, or a home-cooked meal that resonates with local pride. In these intimate settings, you become part of a shared cultural moment—an exchange of warmth and respect that lingers long after you've left.

Navigating the Book

This guide is designed to illuminate Japan's underexplored realms—places where local festivals still shape community life and rural crafts quietly endure. Each chapter offers insights on a particular aspect of the country's tapestry, from the shifting moods of the seasons to lesser-known cityscapes bursting with creativity. While you'll encounter references to famous locations for context, the spotlight remains on lesser-publicized spots that may not appear in mainstream travel guides.

1. **Seasons and Festivities**: Discover how Japan's cyclical transformations—spring blooms, summer festivals, autumn foliage, and winter illuminations—influence both daily life and travel options.

2. **Mountain Hamlets & Coastal Havens**: Step into serene valleys and seaside enclaves largely untouched by mass tourism. These chapters focus on the lifestyles, traditions, and natural wonders found away from urban centers.

3. **Gardens, Nature Reserves & Offbeat Cities**: Wander through sculpted landscapes, wildlife sanctuaries, and hidden urban hubs that combine historical charm with modern art scenes.

4. **Culinary Secrets & More**: Go beyond sushi and ramen to explore the heart of Japan's

food culture—family-run izakayas, underground dining pop-ups, and seasonal specialties that define regional identity.

Beyond the Basics

Each chapter includes practical sidebars and tips on local customs, language pointers, and eco-friendly travel choices. Rather than merely listing destinations, this book invites you to understand **why** these locales matter—to the people who live there and to Japan's cultural heritage as a whole.

How to Use This Guide

- **Savor the Unexpected**: Consider this book a launching pad, not a strict itinerary. The magic of hidden gems often lies in unplanned detours—an abandoned train route, a family-run orchard tour, or a chance to observe a centuries-old festival.

- **Seek Local Voices**: Wherever you roam, engage with the community. Strike up conversations at morning markets, ask a station attendant for walking trail suggestions, or learn about local legends from museum docents. Such exchanges can lead you to discoveries that lie off any pre-mapped route.

- **Travel Responsibly**: Many areas highlighted here rely on small-scale agriculture, artisanal crafts, or fragile ecosystems. Show respect by minimizing waste, being mindful of local etiquettes, and supporting small businesses wherever possible. Embrace each region's traditions with an open mind.

- **Stay Curious**: Hidden gems are a testament to Japan's layered identity—where rural shrines host elaborate rituals, and quiet neighborhoods spawn avant-garde art scenes. The more questions you ask, the richer your experience becomes.

Integrating Practical Tools

Language snippets, cultural etiquette tips, and travel hacks appear in callout boxes or sidebars. Use them to plan day trips, decipher train schedules, or navigate local dialect variations. Feel free to pick and choose what's most relevant to your interests— whether that's nature hikes, community festivals, or gastronomic adventures.

A Journey of Discovery

Ultimately, this book is more than a travel guide; it's an invitation to open your senses to Japan's quieter side. By wandering beyond the typical tourist circuit, you'll sense the heartbeat of communities that still uphold age-old customs—even as they adapt to modern times. You'll taste flavors you never thought possible in humble roadside eateries and witness daily rituals like morning prayers at a shrine where you might be the only visitor.

Connecting with the Land and Its People

Picture yourself in a countryside orchard, learning the delicate art of pear pollination from a farmer whose family has tended these trees for generations. Or imagine strolling through a small-town festival where entire streets light up with lanterns made by local schoolchildren, each telling a piece of the town's story. These encounters form the soul of hidden-gem travel—moments that aren't orchestrated for tourists but arise from a genuine pulse of local life.

Your Role as an Explorer

As you flip through these pages, remember that each destination, each craft, and each tradition represents a living legacy. You become a temporary steward of these worlds, witnessing their beauty and helping to sustain them by being a thoughtful, engaged visitor. In return, these places gift you stories that bridge past and present—a keepsake far more meaningful than any store-bought souvenir.

So pack light, bring an open heart, and ready yourself for the subtle revelations that come when you venture off the usual path. May this guide serve as both compass and companion, leading you to corners of Japan filled with understated wonder and heartfelt connections. Let curiosity be your guide, and embrace the spirit of slow, open-ended exploration—a surefire recipe for a memorable journey.

Yoshida Yuki
Author and Fellow Explorer

Chapter 1: Seasons and Festivities
Mapping Your Adventure

In Japan, the passage of time is intricately woven into the fabric of daily life. The very rhythm of the country depends on the cycle of its four seasons—each bringing unique traditions, culinary delights, and natural wonders that have shaped cultural norms for centuries. In this chapter, we'll dive deeply into how these seasons influence festivals, travel strategies, and the everyday experiences of locals. We'll also discuss regional variations and offer a variety of sample itineraries, guiding you to uncover hidden delights all year round.

1.1 A Land Defined by Seasonal Change

Japan's long, narrow geography stretches from the cold northern reaches of Hokkaido to the subtropical islands of Okinawa. This range means that even within a single month, you might find cherry blossoms blooming in the south while snow still blankets mountainous areas in the north. This stark seasonal contrast not only affects weather patterns, but also provides a cultural tapestry of events, foods, and customs that travelers can explore.

The Cultural Significance of Seasons

1. **Poetry and Art**: Haiku and tanka often reference seasonal elements like sakura (cherry blossoms), momiji (maple leaves), and yuki (snow). Many classical paintings, ceramics, and kimono designs are likewise inspired by the cycles of nature.

2. **Cuisine**: Washoku (traditional Japanese cuisine) is heavily dependent on seasonal ingredients, celebrating the freshest produce available in each region at different times of the year.

3. **Daily Rituals**: Activities such as flower viewing (hanami in spring) or autumn foliage excursions (momijigari) are deeply embedded in the national psyche.

By grasping the broader cultural importance of seasons, visitors can approach each new experience with heightened sensitivity, recognizing the reverence many Japanese hold for nature's constant changes.

1.2 Spring (March–May): Rebirth and Renewal

When people think of Japan in spring, visions of cherry blossoms often come to mind. While sakura season is indeed iconic, there's more to spring than meets the eye. In rural areas, farmers ready their fields for planting; in mountain villages, snow begins to melt, revealing hidden paths that have been inaccessible during winter.

Cherry Blossoms and Beyond

- **Famous vs. Secret Spots**: Tokyo's Ueno Park and Kyoto's Maruyama Park burst with crowds seeking the perfect bloom. To avoid massive throngs, consider visiting smaller towns like Kakunodate in Akita or Hirosaki in Aomori. Both offer spectacular cherry-blossom tunnels flanked by historical architecture.

- **Sakura Culture**: Cherry blossoms symbolize the transient nature of life—a theme deeply rooted in Japanese aesthetics. This concept, known as **mono no aware**, reminds observers to cherish fleeting moments of beauty.

- **Hanami Etiquette**: If you participate in a hanami party (cherry-blossom viewing), be mindful of space, keep noise levels respectful, and dispose of trash properly. Locals often arrive early to reserve spots, so plan accordingly if you're traveling in a group.

Spring Festivals & Local Customs

- **Hina Matsuri (Girls' Day)**: Celebrated on March 3rd, families display ornamental dolls representing the Imperial Court. While it's widely recognized, smaller towns may have unique doll festivals or parades seldom seen by outsiders.

- **Takayama Spring Festival**: The floats (yatai) here are intricately crafted and paraded through the streets, lit by lanterns at night for a mystical atmosphere.

- **Wisteria and Other Blooms**: Beyond sakura, spring also brings wisteria, azaleas, and a variety of other blossoms. Seek out gardens in Ibaraki's Hitachi Seaside Park or Fukuoka's Kawachi Fujien for colorful alternatives.

Practical Spring Travel Tips

1. **Weather Variability**: Early spring can still be chilly, especially in higher elevations. Layer your clothing to adapt to temperature swings.

2. **Crowds**: Late March to mid-April is peak travel time for both domestic and international

tourists chasing cherry blossoms. Booking accommodations and transportation well in advance is crucial.

3. **Local Produce**: Spring vegetables like bamboo shoots, sansai (mountain greens), and fresh strawberries appear in markets. Don't miss these seasonal treats if you're a foodie.

1.3 Summer (June–August): Festivals and Coastal Adventures

As Japan transitions into summer, temperatures climb and the atmosphere becomes electric with the energy of countless festivals. While humidity and the rainy season can deter some, this is actually a fantastic time for more intrepid travelers to venture off the beaten path.

Rainy Season Mystique

- **Tsuyu (Rainy Season)**: Typically lasting from early June to mid-July on Honshu, tsuyu is characterized by intermittent rain and high humidity. Rural areas, with their rice paddies and mist-shrouded forests, take on an otherworldly beauty.

- **Advantages of Tsuyu**: Travel costs can dip slightly during this period. Popular spots are less crowded, and if you enjoy photography, the soft light and reflective puddles create stunning compositions.

Summer Festivals Galore

1. **Obon (Mid-August)**: A time when families honor their ancestors, Obon frequently features bon odori dances at local shrines. While major cities draw bigger crowds, smaller towns often have more intimate celebrations, complete with homegrown dance troupes and a communal atmosphere.

2. **Fireworks (Hanabi Taikai)**: The iconic image of colorful explosions lighting up the night sky is synonymous with a Japanese summer. Some of the most beloved displays are found in smaller locales, offering easier vantage points and friendlier crowds. Consider traveling to places like Omagari in Akita or the Miyajima Fireworks Festival near Hiroshima.

3. **Local Food Stalls (Yatai)**: During summer festivals, streets come alive with vendors selling takoyaki (octopus balls), yakisoba (fried noodles), and shaved ice (kakigōri). Trying these street foods is half the fun!

Beaches and Island Hopping

- **Less-Known Coastal Spots**: Beyond the well-trodden beaches of Okinawa or the Izu

Peninsula, many prefectures on the Sea of Japan side—like Shimane or Yamagata—offer hidden coves and pristine sands relatively undiscovered by foreign tourists.

- **Marine Activities**: Snorkeling, diving, and sea kayaking are popular in areas like the Kerama Islands (Okinawa) or around Shikoku. If you're an avid diver, you'll find coral reefs and abundant marine life in waters that match tropical destinations worldwide.

- **Safety Tips**: Summer in Japan can be hot and humid. Stay hydrated, wear sunscreen, and be mindful of local guidelines on water safety, especially if visiting remote beaches.

1.4 Autumn (September–November): Foliage and Harvest Rituals

Autumn is widely regarded as one of the most visually striking seasons. Temperatures cool to a comfortable range, the humidity of summer dissipates, and Japanese maples ignite hillsides with fiery hues of red and orange.

Nature's Fiery Canvas

- **Beyond Kyoto**: While Kyoto's temples are world-famous for autumn foliage, consider heading to spots like Nikko in Tochigi

Prefecture or Daisen in Tottori Prefecture for equally breathtaking sights with fewer tourists.

- **Momijigari**: The term literally means "red leaf hunting," reflecting the cultural practice of venturing out to admire changing leaves. Many locals plan day trips specifically to see koyo (autumn leaves) at their peak.

Harvest and Community Festivals

- **Rice Harvest**: In many rural communities, harvest time is marked by festivals thanking the gods for a bountiful crop. Expect traditional dances, drum performances, and communal feasts.

- **Sake Breweries**: Autumn is when newly brewed sake starts to become available. Some breweries hold open-house events, allowing visitors to sample varieties straight from the vat.

- **Local Produce**: The seasonal bounty includes chestnuts, persimmons, sweet potatoes, and matsutake mushrooms. Street markets in the countryside often highlight these goodies.

Typhoon Considerations

Early autumn can coincide with typhoon season. Though these storms bring heavy rain and strong winds, they also pass relatively quickly. Always check weather forecasts if traveling in late August or September, especially in coastal or island regions.

1.5 Winter (December–February): Snowy Landscapes and Illuminations

Winter in Japan can range from mild conditions in Kyushu and Okinawa to some of the heaviest snowfall on earth in parts of Tohoku and Hokkaido. For many travelers, the idea of hot springs nestled in snowy forests and glittering winter illuminations is irresistibly romantic.

Embracing the Snow

- **Snow Country Adventures**: Regions like Nagano, Niigata, and Hokkaido offer world-class ski resorts. Even if you're not a skier, you can still enjoy scenic train rides and winter festivals featuring colossal snow sculptures.

- **Onsen Culture**: There's nothing like soaking in a hot spring while snow drifts gently around you. Towns such as Ginzan Onsen in Yamagata or Noboribetsu Onsen in Hokkaido are famed for their steam-filled lanes lined with historical inns.

Illuminations and Festive Cheer

- **Urban Light Displays**: Cities like Tokyo, Osaka, and Kobe host large-scale illumination events. In smaller towns, you might find more modest but equally charming installations along riverbanks or shopping streets.

- **New Year Traditions**: Shōgatsu is Japan's most significant holiday. Besides visiting shrines for Hatsumode, families gather to eat osechi ryōri (special New Year dishes) and ozōni (a mochi soup). Observing or participating in these customs can offer insights into Japanese family life.

Surviving Winter Conditions

- **Layering is Key**: Japanese buildings may or may not have central heating. Layer your clothing and be prepared for temperature changes indoors and outdoors.

- **Transportation Delays**: Heavy snow can disrupt train or plane schedules, especially in northern areas. Always have a backup plan if traveling during peak winter months.

1.6 Regional Variations Worth Noting

While each season has its general patterns, regional quirks add another layer of complexity—and excitement—to traveling in Japan.

- **Tohoku**: Known for harsh winters and brilliant autumn foliage, Tohoku's rural festivals and onsen towns often reward those willing to traverse its quieter roads.

- **Shikoku**: Summers can be quite hot, but spring and autumn are ideal times to walk segments of the 88-temple pilgrimage route or explore Iya Valley's vine bridges.

- **Kyushu**: Early springs and milder winters. Active volcanoes, such as Mt. Aso, and numerous hot spring areas make it fascinating year-round.

- **Okinawa**: Subtropical climate ensures that even winter is comfortable. Typhoons might impact summer travel here more significantly than on mainland Japan.

1.7 Festivals: A Deeper Look

We've touched on some major festivals, but the depth of local matsuri culture deserves more attention.

1. **Hanami Parties**: Not an official "festival," but effectively a nationwide celebration of spring. Families, coworkers, and friends gather under blooming trees to eat, drink, and sing karaoke. Smaller towns have hanami

traditions unique to their local shrines or castle grounds.

2. **Yuki Matsuri (Snow Festivals)**: Beyond Sapporo, towns like Asahikawa, Otaru, and Tokamachi carve out their unique niche with stunning ice lanterns, snow castles, and night illuminations.

3. **Lantern Festivals**: The Nagasaki Lantern Festival during Chinese New Year is a grand spectacle of color and light, deeply influenced by the city's multicultural history. Even lesser-known lantern events in mountainous villages can be mesmerizing.

4. **Harvest and Dance Festivals**: Awa Odori in Tokushima and Gujō Odori in Gifu are two of the most famous dance festivals, but nearly every prefecture has some variant, often featuring local dance steps and costumes passed down through generations.

1.8 Seasonal Travel Strategies

Beyond the basics, here are deeper tactics for maximizing each season's charm:

1. **Follow Local Calendars**: Seasonal peaks for blossoms or foliage can shift depending on weather patterns. Many Japanese websites

track "blooming forecasts" and "koyo forecasts," updated frequently.

2. **Stay in Smaller Towns**: Rather than basing yourself exclusively in big cities, consider booking accommodations in satellite towns or villages. This often provides a quieter and more authentic experience of the season's highlights.

3. **Embrace Off-Peak Travel**: If you can handle a bit of rain or cold, traveling just before or after peak blossom or foliage periods can unveil incredible scenes minus the tourist rush.

4. **Learn Some Language Basics**: Simple Japanese phrases go a long way, especially if you want to learn about local customs or festival times from residents who may not speak English.

5. **Cultural Awareness**: Each season has specific etiquette points—like cleaning up after hanami picnics or following local mores at onsen resorts. Demonstrating respect for these customs can open doors to deeper cultural exchanges.

1.9 Sample Seasonal Itineraries

Spring: Cherry Blossoms & Rural Revival

- **Days 1–3 (Tokyo → Nagano)**: Combine city excitement with quieter onsen towns near Nagano's snow-capped mountains. Try day trips to Matsumoto Castle or Jigokudani Monkey Park if time allows.

- **Days 4–5 (Akita)**: Travel north to Kakunodate, famed for its samurai district blanketed in pink blossoms. Explore well-preserved houses, then stroll along the Hinokinai River lined with cherry trees.

- **Days 6–7 (Sea of Japan Coast)**: Unwind in a coastal fishing village. Sample fresh seafood, visit local morning markets, and absorb the slower pace of life.

Summer: Vibrant Festivals & Hidden Shores

- **Days 1–2 (Gifu Prefecture)**: Experience an intimate Obon festival in Gujō Hachiman. Dance through the night with locals amid lantern-lit streets and gentle river breezes.

- **Days 3–5 (Tottori)**: Go sand-boarding on Tottori's vast dunes, then cool off by exploring the Uradome Coast's clear waters. Try catching your dinner with a local fishing tour.

- **Days 6–7 (Shikoku or Smaller Islands):** Island-hop or savor the quiet beaches of Ehime or Kochi. If you're daring, attempt the Shimanami Kaidō cycling route connecting Hiroshima Prefecture to Ehime.

Autumn: Foliage & Cultural Harvest

- **Days 1–3 (Kansai Region):** Base yourself in Osaka or Kyoto, then take side trips to rural Wakayama. Hike the UNESCO-listed Kumano Kodo pilgrimage trails, lined with vividly colored leaves.

- **Days 4–5 (Tohoku Region):** Venture to Miyagi or Yamagata for their dramatic gorges and onsen towns. Seek out local harvest festivals featuring warm hospitality and seasonal dishes.

- **Days 6–7 (Niigata or Nagano):** Sample newly harvested rice and sake, witness farmers in the fields, and possibly join a harvest event if your timing aligns.

Winter: Snow Country & Onsen Escapes

- **Days 1–3 (Hokkaido):** Start in Sapporo for the Snow Festival. If crowds get overwhelming, move on to smaller ski towns like Niseko or Furano for powdery slopes or quieter winter activities.

- **Days 4–5 (Akita)**: Head south to witness the Namahage Sedo Festival, where costumed deities descend upon local homes. Warm up at Nyuto Onsen's rustic hot spring baths.

- **Days 6–7 (Tokyo & Surroundings)**: Return to a capital city transformed by winter illuminations. If you prefer calmer vibes, consider a smaller Kanto town like Nikko or Hakone for final onsen relaxation.

1.10 Chapter 1 Summary

Japan's four seasons infuse every corner of the country with distinct character—shaping festivals, flavors, and the very essence of daily life. By understanding the nuances of each season, you can tailor your journey to witness not only iconic sights but also lesser-known treasures often overlooked by mass tourism. From the quiet of a rainy-season temple in Kyoto to the boisterous energy of a rural Obon dance, these seasonal experiences bind travelers to Japan's cultural heartbeat.

Coming Up Next: In Chapter 2, we'll venture into Japan's **mountain villages**, where centuries-old traditions and breathtaking natural beauty converge. These hidden hamlets allow visitors to disconnect from modern rush and reconnect with the country's agrarian roots, offering a deeper, more authentic view of Japanese life.

Chapter 2: Quiet Villages in the Mountains

If Japan's seasons guide the country's annual rhythm, then its mountain villages are the soul that has quietly persisted through centuries of change. High-altitude hamlets preserve older ways of life, from communal farm work to generation-spanning festivals, all set against stunning backdrops of towering peaks, terraced rice fields, and winding rivers. In this extended chapter, we delve deep into these rural enclaves, learning how they've shaped—and been shaped by—Japan's history and cultural identity.

2.1 Discovering Mountain Life: A Retreat from Modernity

The Quiet Allure of Rural Japan

Far from the neon canyons of Tokyo or Osaka, life in mountainous regions flows at a gentler pace. The air is crisp, the sounds of nature more pronounced, and time seems to slow. For many locals, traditions like mochi pounding (kagami mochi) for the New Year or lighting bonfires on cold winter nights aren't mere pageantry—they're part of sustaining cultural memory.

Why Seek Out Mountain Villages?

1. **Cultural Preservation**: Many rural communities still practice age-old crafts such as lacquerware, papermaking, or straw sandal weaving.

2. **Seasonal Harmony**: Residents adapt their lives to the changing landscape—planting in spring, tending rice paddies in summer, harvesting in autumn, and finding comfort in hot springs during winter.

3. **Deep Hospitality**: Visitors often find themselves treated as honored guests, invited into family-run minshuku (guesthouses) and introduced to local customs rarely seen by outsiders.

Historical Roots

*   **Edo-Era Isolation**: During the Edo period (1603–1868), traveling between domains was heavily regulated. Mountain villages often developed unique dialects, customs, and architectural styles due to geographical and political isolation.

- **Post-Town Legacy**: Some mountain settlements served as post towns (shukuba) along ancient highways like the Nakasendo or Tokaido. Vestiges of these routes remain, offering glimpses into a time when travel was mostly on foot or horseback.

- **Modern Challenges**: With the rise of urbanization, younger generations have moved to cities, leaving older residents to maintain centuries of tradition. Tourism can provide a lifeline, helping preserve local heritage and infrastructure.

2.2 Shirakawa-go and Gokayama: Icons of Alpine Heritage

No discussion of mountain villages is complete without mentioning **Shirakawa-go** (Gifu Prefecture) and **Gokayama** (Toyama Prefecture). Both are UNESCO World Heritage Sites thanks to their distinctive **gassho-zukuri** farmhouses. But beyond their postcard beauty, these areas offer an immersion into a bygone era.

Gassho-Zukuri Farmhouses

- **Architecture**: The steep thatched roofs, resembling hands pressed in prayer, were designed for harsh winters with heavy snow. Inside, multiple levels often housed silkworm-

30

raising operations—a vital industry historically.

- **Living Museums**: Some farmhouses operate as folk museums, displaying traditional hearths (irori), agricultural tools, and crafts. Others remain private homes or minshuku, where overnight guests can experience local family life.

- **Community Spirit**: Thatching roofs is a communal event; villagers come together to replace them in a practice that can take days of collective effort.

Seasonal Highlights

- **Spring & Summer**: Fields and mountainsides burst with color, with wildflowers blooming around farmhouses. Locally grown vegetables, like sansai (mountain greens), become table staples.

- **Autumn**: Fiery foliage frames the rustic architecture, and harvest festivals see villagers offering thanks for the year's bounty.

- **Winter**: Few sights are as enchanting as snow-laden gassho-zukuri homes illuminated at night—a scene reminiscent of a fairy-tale landscape.

Responsible Tourism

Due to increasing popularity, these villages can become crowded during peak seasons. Travelers are encouraged to:

1. **Stay Overnight**: Instead of rushing through, consider a minshuku stay. Evenings and early mornings are magical times, when day-trippers have left.

2. **Respect Private Property**: Not every farmhouse is open to the public. Look for signage indicating whether you can enter or photograph certain areas.

3. **Support Local Shops**: Purchasing souvenirs from resident artisans or sampling local produce helps keep these communities thriving.

2.3 Kiso Valley: Echoes of the Edo Era
Tsumago and Magome: Gateway Towns

Straddling Nagano and Gifu Prefectures, the Kiso Valley formed a major part of the **Nakasendo**, one of the five major routes linking Edo (old Tokyo) with Kyoto. Here, time appears frozen:

- **Stone-Paved Streets**: Tsumago and Magome have meticulously preserved Edo-period architecture. No overhead cables mar the skyline, and vehicles are restricted in certain areas to keep the historical ambiance intact.

- **Post-Town Culture**: Historically, these towns provided lodging and supplies to travelers. Even now, ryokan and teahouses welcome modern visitors with the same spirit of hospitality that supported weary samurai and merchants centuries ago.

- **Trail Hiking**: A 7–8 km stretch of wooded trail connects the two towns. Lush in summer, fiery in autumn, and serene in winter, it offers a literal walk through history. Occasional roadside teahouses serve light refreshments.

Seasonal Events and Activities

- **Summer Lantern Nights**: Local residents hang lanterns outside homes and shops, recreating the soft glow that would have guided travelers by night.

- **Edo-Themed Parades**: Periodically, the towns host reenactments complete with people in samurai or merchant attire, adding a sense of festival to the cobblestone streets.

Travel Tip: While you can day-trip from Nagoya or Matsumoto, consider staying a night in Tsumago or Magome to appreciate the quiet after most tourists depart. Early morning strolls reveal mist-shrouded mountains and almost ethereal solitude.

2.4 Beyond Honshu: Kyushu's Alpine Retreats

Kurokawa Onsen (Kumamoto Prefecture)

Kyushu's mountainous heartland is rich in hot springs, with **Kurokawa Onsen** being one of the most celebrated. The local emphasis on harmony with nature permeates everything from the town's architecture to its lighting (discreet lanterns instead of glaring neon).

- **Onsen Culture**: A visitor pass (nyuto tegata) allows you to try multiple rotenburo (open-air baths). Some are nestled beside rivers, others perched on higher ground overlooking forests.

- **Seasonal Charm**: In summer, the night sky sparkles with fireflies near the waterways. Come autumn, the surrounding woods blaze in red and gold. Winter sees steam rising against a snowy backdrop.

- **Local Foods**: Don't miss local specialties such as horse meat (basashi) or dengaku (vegetables and tofu coated in miso and grilled over an open fire), often served in cozy ryokan dining rooms.

Other Kyushu Mountain Villages

- **Takachiho (Miyazaki Prefecture)**: Known for its lush gorge and nightly kagura performances at local shrines—a dramatic form of Shinto dance that retells ancient myths.

- **Mount Aso Region**: Dotted with farmland and smaller onsen villages. The caldera itself is one of the largest in the world, offering remarkable hiking and horseback riding opportunities.

2.5 The Iya Valley: Shikoku's Hidden Frontier

Often referred to as one of Japan's "Three Great Unexplored Regions," the **Iya Valley** in Tokushima Prefecture boasts deep gorges, vine bridges (kazurabashi), and remote farm stays.

A Landscape Like No Other

- **Vine Bridges**: Originally woven from vines to deter invaders, these swaying structures now draw adventurous travelers seeking a rush—and jaw-dropping canyon views.

- **Outdoor Activities**: White-water rafting on the Yoshino River is world-class, and the winding roads through the valley are popular among cyclists.

- **Isolation and Myths**: Legend says the Heike clan took refuge here after defeat in the Genpei War (12th century), and remnants of that era's history still permeate local lore.

Cultural Note: The region's isolation has led to unique dialects and folktales. English signage can be minimal, so a translation app or phrasebook is often essential.

2.6 Hands-On Experiences in Mountain Hamlets

Farm Stays and WWOOFing

For those seeking immersion, programs like **WWOOF** (World Wide Opportunities on Organic Farms) arrange volunteer stays at local farms. You might help plant rice, tend to vegetable gardens, or learn to craft miso. Even if you're not volunteering, smaller guesthouses often welcome help with routine tasks, fostering meaningful exchanges and deeper cultural understanding.

Craft Workshops

- **Washi Paper in Gifu**: Many workshops demonstrate traditional paper-making techniques using mulberry bark. Participants leave with personalized sheets or even small crafts.

- **Woodcarving and Lacquerware**: In mountainous areas with abundant forests, these crafts have flourished for centuries. Check local tourism offices for workshop schedules.

- **Soba Making**: Buckwheat noodles are a staple in colder regions. Under the guidance of local experts, you'll knead, roll, and cut dough into noodles—a surprisingly meditative process.

Seasonal Festivals and Rituals

- **Snow Festivals**: Some remote villages carve small igloos or light candlelit snow tunnels, a more intimate counterpart to big city events. Interacting with the local families who organize them is often a highlight.

- **Autumn Harvest Celebrations**: In these close-knit communities, everyone pitches in to harvest rice, mushrooms, or chestnuts. The ensuing festival might feature taiko drumming, sake tasting, and communal meals.

- **Shinto Ceremonies**: Small shrines hold their own yearly matsuri, inviting residents and visitors to share in prayers for health, abundance, and protection from natural disasters.

2.7 Practical Tips for Mountain Travel

1. **Transportation**: Rural bus and train schedules may be infrequent. Plan ahead or consider renting a car if you're comfortable driving on narrow, winding roads.

2. **Cash is King**: Many isolated areas don't accept credit cards. Stock up on yen before heading into more remote regions.

3. **Language**: Basic Japanese phrases go a long way. Locals are often excited to meet travelers and share stories, but English proficiency may be limited.

4. **Weather Preparedness**: Mountain weather is unpredictable. Pack layers, rain gear, and sturdy footwear if you plan to hike or explore the outdoors.

5. **Etiquette**: Greeting elders with a slight bow, removing shoes when entering homes or ryokan, and respecting communal spaces at onsen can leave a positive impression.

2.8 Spotlight: Lesser-Known Alpine Gems

- **Oku-Aizu (Fukushima Prefecture)**: Known for deep snow in winter and breathtaking gold hues in autumn. Local crafts include lacquerware and a unique form of weaving.

- **Miyama (Kyoto Prefecture)**: Thatched-roof houses, known as kayabuki, line tranquil roads. It offers a stark contrast to the hustle of central Kyoto, yet remains within day-trip distance.

- **Nagano's Snow Villages**: Beyond famous ski resorts like Hakuba, smaller villages boast lesser-known slopes and welcoming minshuku with fewer crowds.

2.9 Chapter 2 Summary

From the UNESCO-listed gassho-zukuri farmhouses of Shirakawa-go to the secluded hot springs of Kyushu's Kurokawa Onsen, Japan's mountain villages provide an intimate look into the country's historical and cultural tapestry. Here, you'll witness a lifestyle in sync with the seasons, guided by communal bonds and sustained by unwavering traditions.

By stepping into these hidden hamlets, travelers do more than just appreciate picturesque scenery; they gain access to centuries of wisdom about coexistence with nature, meaningful social ties, and creative resilience in the face of modernization. Whether you're marveling at a snow-covered rooftop in Gokayama, partaking in harvest festivals in the Kiso Valley, or forging new friendships in a volunteer program, the heart of Japan beats strongest in its highland enclaves.

Next Stop: Chapter 3 focuses on **Coastal Escapes and Hidden Beaches**, where you'll trade the hush of mountain forests for the whisper of waves. If you've ever dreamt of discovering undiscovered coves or forgotten fishing villages, you're about to embark on a seaside journey that matches the enchantment found in the highlands.

Chapter 3: Coastal Escapes and Hidden Beaches

For a country surrounded by ocean on all sides, Japan boasts a remarkably diverse range of coastal environments—from the rugged, windswept shores of Hokkaido to the subtropical beaches of Okinawa. While busy port cities and popular resort destinations often capture the limelight, there's a far quieter side to Japan's coasts. In this chapter, we'll delve deeply into remote fishing villages, pristine stretches of shoreline, and island communities that remain blissfully under-traveled, offering a serene escape into authentic maritime culture.

3.1 The Diversity of Japan's Coastlines
Four Main Bodies of Water

1. **Sea of Japan (West Coast)**

    o **Varied Landscape**: Expect cooler
       waters, dramatic cliffs, and pebble
       beaches, though you'll find sandy
       stretches near certain bays. Heavy
       snowfall in winter can transform the
       coastline into a silent, snow-blanketed
       realm—an ideal retreat if you enjoy
       chilly solitude.

    o **Cultural Traits**: Many communities on
       the Sea of Japan coast have long-
       standing traditions of boat-building, sea
       salt production, and winter festivals
       designed to celebrate (or appease) the
       region's challenging weather.

2. **Pacific Ocean (East Coast)**

    o **Modern & Traditional**: Regions closer
       to Tokyo and Yokohama often blend
       bustling urban life with scenic beaches
       popular for day-trips or weekend
       getaways.

    o **Surfing Hotspots**: Stronger waves in
       Chiba (Kujūkuri Beach) and parts of
       Ibaraki attract surfers, while quieter
       coves in Shizuoka or the Izu Peninsula
       offer calmer waters and fewer crowds.

3. **Seto Inland Sea (Between Honshu, Shikoku, and Kyushu)**

   o **Archipelago Wonders**: Thousands of small islands (many uninhabited) dot this tranquil waterway. The mild climate and gentle tides encourage cycling tours, leisurely ferry rides, and a culture of inter-island travel.

   o **Sea-to-Table Cuisine**: The calm waters support fisheries for oysters, sea bream, and other local delicacies. You'll often find small seaside shacks serving seafood fresh off the boat.

4. **East China Sea (Southwest of Kyushu and Okinawa)**

   o **Tropical & Subtropical Zones**: This warmer region is home to coral reefs, mangrove forests, and white-sand beaches—offering year-round marine activities like scuba diving, snorkeling, and whale-watching.

   o **Cultural Melting Pot**: Historically, trade routes linked Okinawa with Southeast Asia and China, influencing local cuisine, language, and customs.

Unique Coastal Climates

- **Northern Prefectures**: Along the Sea of Japan side in Akita or Aomori, the mercury rarely soars even in summer. Wind-swept beaches and fishing wharfs take on a windswept, solitary beauty, perfect for reflection and long walks.

- **Central Japan**: Shonan in Kanagawa is famous among surfers, while pockets of Shizuoka's coastline—like around Shimoda—boast hidden coves often overlooked by tourists rushing to more famous spots.

- **Southern Islands**: Okinawa, Kagoshima, and the Amami archipelago promise lush greenery, vibrant coral reefs, and a pace of life that unfolds under swaying palm trees.

3.2 Hidden Fishing Villages and Their Allure

The Rhythms of Coastal Life

Away from the neon of urban Japan, fishing villages embody a timeless routine: sunrise sees fishermen casting off, midday markets teem with fresh catches, and by evening, the community gathers to share meals and stories. This cyclical existence is deeply rooted in Shinto beliefs that revere the sea as both provider and unpredictable force.

1. **Daily Catch**: From amberjack in Kagoshima to sea urchin in northern Hokkaido, local specialties vary widely depending on climate and ocean currents. In many villages, you can watch fishermen sort and prepare their haul on rustic piers—a spectacle few urbanites witness.

2. **Local Festivities**: Festivals often revolve around thanksgiving for the sea's bounty. You might witness boat blessings (where priests pray for safety and plentiful fish), raucous drumming along the docks, or nighttime processions of lantern-lit boats forming a chain of light on the water.

3. **Culinary Traditions**: Beyond sushi and sashimi, coastal villages have unique dishes like ishikari-nabe (salmon stew) in Hokkaido or arajiru (fish-head soup) in southwestern prefectures. Eating locally fished seafood hours after it's caught is an unforgettable gastronomic experience.

Notable Villages to Explore

- **Ine (Kyoto Prefecture)**
    - **Funaya Boathouses**: These structures are half-home, half-boat storage, fronting directly on the sea.

Some are centuries old and have been passed down through generations.

- o **Village Strolls**: Narrow lanes line the waterfront, offering glimpses into daily life—fishermen mending nets or elderly residents tending seaside gardens.

- **Ama Town (Oki Islands, Shimane Prefecture)**

  - o **Remote Archipelago**: The Oki Islands remain relatively unknown to mass tourism, preserving an island culture that has endured for centuries.

  - o **Seaweed Farming**: Konbu (kelp) and wakame are staple seaweeds harvested here, forming the basis of myriad soups and side dishes.

- **Hachijō-jima (Tokyo Prefecture)**

  - o **Volcanic Landscape**: The island's rugged black-sand beaches contrast with dense tropical flora. Scuba divers can explore lava-formed reefs teeming with vibrant fish.

  - o **Island Cuisine**: Local delicacies include kusaya (fermented fish) and ashitaba tempura (a leafy green unique to the region). The bold flavors might challenge newcomers, but they speak to the island's heritage.

Insider Tip: For spontaneous travelers, consider checking local harbors in the early morning. Sometimes fishermen offer rides on their boats for a small fee—an offbeat way to experience daily life on the sea.

3.3 Remote Beaches and Island Adventures

Underrated Coastal Hideaways

1. **Noto Peninsula (Ishikawa Prefecture)**

   o **Traditional Salt Farms**: Artisanal salt-making along the coast has continued for generations. You can watch—or even participate in—processes that involve evaporating seawater on large flat pans.

   o **Wajima Morning Market**: If you visit Wajima city, explore its famed market for fresh seafood, lacquerware, and produce from surrounding fields.

2. **Gunkanjima (Nagasaki Prefecture)**

   o **Hashima Island's History**: A coal-mining powerhouse until the 1970s,

Gunkanjima's towering concrete apartments now stand in eerie ruin. Coastal tours weave around the island, highlighting the stark contrast between open sea and abandoned high-rises.

- **Sustainability Lessons**: Gunkanjima is also a cautionary tale of rapid industrial boom and bust—an intriguing stop for travelers interested in environmental and social history.

3. **Tottori Sand Dunes (Tottori Prefecture)**

- **Beyond the Dunes**: Though the sweeping dunes get most of the attention, nearby areas feature small onsen towns, wild coastlines, and hidden rock formations carved by strong sea winds.

- **Sand Museum**: Tottori's Sand Museum hosts elaborate sand-sculpture exhibits from international artists, offering a quirky cultural addition to the coastal adventure.

The Okinawan Escape

When discussing Japanese beaches, Okinawa inevitably surfaces. Yet, beyond the main island's bustling resort areas, a constellation of smaller islands—each with distinct charm—awaits.

- **Zamami Island**

  - **Kerama Blue**: The clear waters around the Kerama Islands are famously referred to as "Kerama Blue" for their dazzling hue. Ideal for spotting clownfish, sea turtles, and mesmerizing coral gardens.

  - **Slow Pace**: A single village anchors Zamami; many residents know each other by name, giving the entire island a welcoming vibe.

- **Ishigaki and Taketomi Islands**

  - **Ryukyuan Legacy**: Traces of the old Ryukyu Kingdom remain in local dialects, architecture, and festivals, distinct from mainland Japan's culture.

  - **Nature Highlights**: Ishigaki's mangrove forests host kayaking tours; Taketomi's star-sand beaches fascinate beachcombers with tiny, star-shaped shells.

Marine Life and Eco-Friendly Travel

- **Snorkeling and Diving**

  - **Coral Gardens**: From the coral reefs of Miyako-jima to the sunken shipwrecks near Yonaguni, snorkelers and divers encounter vibrant underwater worlds. Many local tour operators practice reef-safe guidelines.

- **Seasonal Marine Visitors**: Whale sharks occasionally appear off Okinawan coasts, while humpback whales frequent the Kerama Islands in winter.

- **Beach Cleanups**

  - **Community Spirit**: In some villages, weekly or monthly cleanups foster a sense of collective stewardship over the environment. Tourists who pitch in often form lasting friendships with residents.

  - **Plastic Pollution Awareness**: Beach litter can quickly accumulate due to currents. Engaging in cleanups is a direct way to help and better understand the challenges local communities face.

3.4 Cultural Gems Along the Coast
Art, Architecture, and Cyclists' Paradise

1. **Shimanami Kaidō (Hiroshima–Ehime)**

- o **Island-Hopping by Bike**: Spanning roughly 70 kilometers, the route links Honshu to Shikoku via bridges that arc over scenic straits. Cyclists can break up the journey by overnighting in small fishing towns or visiting roadside cafés serving citrus-based sweets.

- o **Local Culture**: Each island has a distinct identity—one might be famous for oranges, another for shipbuilding or pottery. The slow pace invites deeper interactions with locals.

2. **Sea Firefly Viewing**

- o **Natural Light Shows**: Under the right conditions, microscopic plankton emit bioluminescent sparks, painting the shoreline with a surreal blue glow.

- o **Where to Find Them**: Locations vary by season, but certain coves in Okayama, Hiroshima, and even parts of Shikoku occasionally host guided tours. Some local inns may let you know the best nights to watch.

Preserving Maritime Heritage

3. **Local Craft and Food Culture**

- **Salting & Fermenting**: Traditional methods like himono (salt-drying fish) or funazushi (fermented crucian carp) demonstrate how communities preserved protein before refrigeration.

- **Boat-Building**: Wooden boat carpentry is still practiced in pockets of Japan, notably in places like Toba (Mie Prefecture) and along some parts of Shikoku's coast. Artisans often share stories of their craft's multi-generational lineage.

3.5 Tips for Coastal Exploration

1. **Check Tides and Weather**

   - **Tidal Shifts**: In some areas, low tide exposes dramatic rock formations or intertidal zones bustling with marine life. High tide may be better for swimming or launching kayaks.

   - **Seasonal Storms**: Typhoons can strike between late summer and early autumn, particularly affecting Okinawa and Kyushu. Always monitor local advisories.

2. **Transportation**

o **Sparse Public Transit**: Many secluded beaches have minimal bus service. A rental car or bicycle can grant more freedom to explore off-grid shorelines.

o **Island Hopping**: Ferry schedules vary widely, and cancellations can occur during rough seas. Having extra flexibility in your travel plan is crucial.

3. **Respect Marine Life**

o **Coral Preservation**: Wearing reef-safe sunscreen (zinc-based, free of harmful chemicals) helps protect coral ecosystems.

o **No Touch Rule**: Resist the urge to pick up starfish, corals, or other creatures. Even small interactions can disrupt fragile habitats.

4. **Stay Hydrated**

o **Summer Heat**: Japanese summers can be punishingly hot, especially on beaches with limited shade. Bring enough water, a hat, and reapply sunscreen often.

o **Local Drinks**: Don't miss sampling unique coastal beverages—from shikuwasa juice in Okinawa to locally brewed craft beers near port towns.

5. **Engage with Locals**

   o **Morning Markets**: Coastal towns often have early markets where fishermen and farmers sell their daily harvest. Casual chats can reveal secret coves or lesser-known festival dates.

   o **Language Tips**: Even a few Japanese phrases—like "Konnichiwa" (hello) or "Arigatō" (thank you)—warmly break the ice.

3.6 Chapter 3 Summary

Japan's coastlines stand as a testament to the country's geographic and cultural richness. Though glossy magazines may highlight high-end Okinawan resorts or surfers flocking to Shonan, countless lesser-known shores hold stories of enduring traditions, communal bonds, and symbiotic relationships with the sea. Whether you find yourself sampling freshly caught squid in a remote fishing village or cycling across island bridges under golden sunsets, the coast promises a side of Japan that is both enthralling and deeply tranquil.

In the next chapter, we'll leave the salt air behind for Japan's **gardens and nature reserves**, where artful landscaping and wild conservation areas coexist to embody a centuries-old commitment to living in harmony with nature. Prepare to explore meticulously pruned pines, moss-draped paths, and quiet forest sanctuaries.

Chapter 4: Serenity in Gardens and Nature Reserves

Japan's scenic wonders aren't limited to towering peaks and rugged coasts; some of its most enchanting vistas lie in the curated elegance of its gardens and the unspoiled sanctity of its national parks. This chapter takes a closer look at these man-made and natural havens, revealing not just their beauty, but also their cultural significance and the philosophy that shapes them.

4.1 A Brief History of Japanese Gardening

From Imperial Estates to Zen Temples

1. **Heian Period (794–1185)**

   - **Courtly Aesthetics**: Aristocrats constructed expansive villa gardens with ponds and islands modeled after

Chinese landscapes. Poetry, music, and moon-viewing formed part of the garden's social functions.

- o **Seasonal Celebrations**: Cherry blossoms in spring, lotus flowers in summer, and autumn maples turned these gardens into ever-evolving stages for court events.

2. **Zen Influence (Kamakura and Muromachi Periods)**

- o **Rock Gardens**: The minimalist karesansui style emerged, using gravel, sand, and carefully placed rocks to evoke entire landscapes in microcosm. Each element holds symbolic value—mountains, rivers, islands.

- o **Meditative Purpose**: These gardens provided backdrops for monks' contemplation, with visitors encouraged to observe from a single vantage point, pondering the nature of impermanence.

3. **Edo Period (1603–1868)**

- o **Daimyō Rivalries**: Feudal lords vied to create the most impressive strolling gardens. Designed with pathways revealing carefully orchestrated scenes at each turn, they often replicated famous sites around Asia on a smaller scale.

- o **Public Spaces**: Some gardens opened to the public during festivals, contributing to a blossoming urban culture centered on leisure, art, and seasonal appreciation.

Principles of Japanese Garden Design

- **Shakkei (Borrowed Scenery)**: Incorporating existing topography or distant landmarks—such as a mountain peak or temple roof—into the garden's composition to expand its perceived space.

- **Asymmetry and Balance**: Rejecting strict symmetry in favor of natural flow. Stones, plants, and water features are arranged to evoke an organic yet harmonious feel.

- **Seasonal Contrast**: Carefully selected vegetation ensures that each season brings unique highlights—lush moss in the rainy season, fiery maples in autumn, camellias in winter, and fresh azaleas in spring.

Cultural Note: Traditionally, Japanese gardens bridge the human and the divine. They invite stillness, reflection, and an awareness of the ephemeral quality of life.

4.2 City Gardens and Hidden Urban Oases

Tokyo's Surprising Green Spaces

1. **Koishikawa Kōrakuen**

   o **Historic Layering**: Established by the Tokugawa clan, it seamlessly merges Chinese-inspired design with local Edo aesthetics. Each bend in the path offers a new vignette—be it a stone bridge or a hidden grove of irises.

   o **Seasonal Delights**: Plum blossoms herald early spring, while maples offer a riot of red in late autumn. Even winter has its charms, with stark silhouettes against tranquil ponds.

2. **Hamarikyu Gardens**

   o **Tidal Pond**: Fed directly by Tokyo Bay, the pond's water level shifts with the tide. This dynamic element ties the garden to the rhythm of the city's maritime past.

   o **Teahouse on the Island**: Savor a bowl of matcha while overlooking waterfowl and distant skyscrapers—a living contrast of old and new Tokyo.

3. **Rikugien**

   o **Literary Inspiration**: Built as a "garden of six poems," Rikugien incorporates scenes drawn from classic Japanese poetry. Strolling its winding paths is akin to meandering through a literary tapestry.

   o **Illuminations**: In autumn, the garden extends visiting hours after dark, bathing the maple and ginkgo leaves in ethereal light.

Kyoto's Temple Gardens

- **Ryoan-ji**

  o **Famous Rock Garden**: The arrangement of stones invites endless interpretation; some see islands in a sea, others see peaks emerging from clouds.

  o **Quiet Reflection**: Arrive early or close to closing time to appreciate the serenity without large tour groups.

- **Ginkaku-ji (Silver Pavilion)**

- **Spiritual Austerity**: Despite its name, Ginkaku-ji was never coated in silver. Instead, it embraces wabi-sabi—a beauty in simplicity and imperfection.

- **Moss Gardens**: The surrounding grounds feature meticulously tended moss carpets, winding streams, and sculpted shrubs.

- **Hidden Gems**

  - **Daitoku-ji's Sub-temples**: Each sub-temple might house its own Zen garden. Visiting them can feel like stepping into private sanctuaries where the hustle of Kyoto fades away.

Osaka, Nagoya, and Beyond

- **Osaka Castle Park**

  - **Seasonal Blooms**: Cherry blossoms line the outer moat, while plums fill orchards with pink and white blossoms in late winter. Summer festivals often set up stalls within the castle grounds.

  - **Nishinomaru Garden**: Adjacent to the castle, it offers a vantage point for photographing the fortress rising behind green lawns or blooming trees.

- **Tokugawa Garden (Nagoya)**

- **Legacy of the Tokugawa Clan**: Once part of the clan's residence, the garden features a large pond circled by waterfalls, rocky outcroppings, and a refurbished teahouse.

- **Cultural Exhibitions**: The on-site museum occasionally hosts exhibitions of samurai armor or traditional arts, adding historical context to your visit.

4.3 Nature Reserves and National Parks
Japan's Commitment to Conservation

With a network of 34 national parks and numerous prefectural reserves, Japan demonstrates a longstanding dedication to preserving wild habitats. These areas protect everything from alpine tundra in the far north to coral reefs in the far south, offering endless possibilities for nature lovers.

1. **Yakushima (Kagoshima Prefecture)**

   - **Enchanted Forests**: Ancient cedars (yakusugi) like Jōmon Sugi, estimated to be over 2,000 years old, tower in mist-laden forests. Moss-draped trunks and hidden waterfalls create an almost otherworldly setting.

- Wildlife Encounters: Troops of macaques and herds of deer roam freely. Some visitors trek multi-day routes, staying in mountain huts to witness sunrise over primeval canopies.

2. **Shiretoko Peninsula (Hokkaido)**

    - **Remote Wilderness**: Often cited as one of Japan's last truly wild frontiers, Shiretoko's steep cliffs and dense forests are home to brown bears, foxes, and salmon-filled rivers.

    - **Drift Ice in Winter**: From late January to early March, ice floes drift down from the Sea of Okhotsk. Tour boats let you experience the surreal sight of eagles perched on ice chunks.

3. **Oze National Park (Gunma, Fukushima, Niigata)**

    - **Wetland Ecosystem**: Boardwalks snake through high-altitude marshes, ensuring minimal human impact. Skunk cabbage blooms in spring, while autumn grasses turn the marsh a warm gold.

    - **Mountain Scenery**: Surrounding peaks reflect off the marsh's shallow waters, making for painterly vistas during sunrise or sunset.

Experiencing Wildlife Ethically

- **Bear Awareness**: While bear encounters remain uncommon, certain trails recommend carrying bear bells. Rangers offer up-to-date information on recent sightings.

- **Respect for Habitat**: This includes leaving no litter behind and refraining from feeding animals, which can disrupt their natural foraging behavior.

- **Local Guides**: Hiring guides not only ensures safety but enriches the experience with ecological insights, folklore, and hidden vantage points.

4.4 Forest Bathing and Reconnecting with Nature

The Concept of Shinrin-yoku

Coined in the 1980s, **shinrin-yoku** (forest bathing) encourages visitors to immerse themselves in nature slowly and intentionally—letting the sights, sounds, and smells of the forest wash over them. Scientific studies suggest such exposure lowers stress hormones and elevates mood.

- **Popular Forest Bathing Spots**: Nikko National Park (Tochigi Prefecture) boasts cedar-lined roads leading to serene shrines, while Akita's beech forests around Shirakami-Sanchi (another UNESCO site) are ideal for quiet, meditative strolls.

- **Guided Sessions**: Some nature centers run forest therapy tours, combining gentle hiking with breathing exercises and mindful observation. These can culminate in a tea ceremony or a short journaling session amid the trees.

Spiritual Connection

In Shinto tradition, forests and mountains have long been believed to house kami (deities). Many shrines nestle in old-growth woods, their pathways flanked by towering cedars. Visitors often describe a palpable sense of tranquility, as if stepping onto sacred ground outside the temporal world.

- **Sacred Groves**: Locations like the vast forest surrounding Togakushi Shrine in Nagano or the towering cryptomeria near Murakami's shrines in Niigata are believed to be charged with spiritual energy.

- **Rituals and Festivals**: Some communities hold annual ceremonies to honor the guardian spirits of the forest, reaffirming bonds between people and nature.

4.5 Off-the-Beaten-Path Gardens and Reserves

Adachi Museum of Art (Shimane Prefecture)

- **Living Paintings**: The garden's design is meticulously maintained—every pebble, tree, and shrub placed to create a harmonious scene viewed from specific angles. Large picture windows inside the museum function like framed art.

- **Seasonal Reflections**: From the exuberance of spring azaleas to the hushed tones of a snow-covered winter tableau, each shift in weather alters the garden's "painting."

Kanazawa's Kenrokuen (Ishikawa Prefecture)

- **Six Attributes**: The garden name references spaciousness, seclusion, artistry, history, water features, and broad vistas. Each corner might present a new element: an old stone lantern, a quiet pond, or a distant tree line borrowed via shakkei.

- **Nearby Cultural Spots**: After wandering Kenrokuen, stroll the Higashi Chaya geisha district or visit the 21st Century Museum of

Contemporary Art for a contrast between traditional and modern aesthetics.

Uncharted Greens

- **Suizen-ji Jōju-en (Kumamoto)**

    o **Landscape Miniatures**: The garden re-creates famous places in miniature form, including a small Mt. Fuji mound. A leisurely circuit showcases each "scene" from different viewpoints.

    o **Spring-Water Tea**: The site's spring-fed lake supplies water for tea ceremonies, reputedly giving the brew a uniquely refreshing taste.

- **Kōraku-en (Okayama)**

    o **Diverse Features**: The sprawling lawns, teahouse, and quaint shrines spread across more than 13 hectares. A small rice paddy fosters an agricultural link—visitors can see how rice is grown and harvested.

    o **Evening Enchantments**: Occasional light-up events let you experience the garden's carefully sculpted landscapes under lanterns and moonlight.

4.6 Practical Tips for Garden and Nature-Reserve Visits

1. **Timing**

    o **Avoid Peak Hours**: Major gardens see crowds in mid-morning or early afternoon, especially during cherry blossom and autumn foliage seasons. Consider an early start or go just before closing.

    o **Night Illuminations**: Some gardens and parks open after dusk on special occasions, offering a mystical experience—lanterns or spotlights highlight key features, creating enchanting silhouettes.

2. **Mind the Seasons**

    o **Blossom Calendars**: Online resources track cherry, plum, wisteria, and azalea bloom progress across Japan, helping you target peak viewing times.

    o **Foliage Reports**: Similar forecasts exist for koyo (autumn leaves), ensuring you don't miss the most vibrant displays.

3. **Entrance Fees**

- Value in Preservation: Fees help maintain historical gardens and parks. Some offer combo tickets for nearby museums or cultural sites, saving money if you plan multiple visits.

- Annual Passes: If you're staying in one city for an extended period, ask about membership options at major gardens.

4. **Rules and Etiquette**

- Stay on Paths: Particularly in moss gardens or preserved wetlands, stepping off marked trails can cause irreparable damage.

- Quiet Atmosphere: Zen gardens and national parks often expect hushed voices, especially around prayer sites.

5. **Combine with Cultural Activities**

- Tea Ceremonies: Many gardens have teahouses offering matcha and sweets. Participating in a short ceremony enriches the sensory experience— aroma, taste, and scenery meld into one moment.

- Volunteer Opportunities: Some reserves welcome volunteers for tree planting or trail upkeep. It's a unique way to engage more deeply with the environment.

4.7 Chapter 4 Summary

From the meandering paths of Edo-period strolling gardens to the untamed splendor of UNESCO-listed forests, Japan's commitment to weaving nature into everyday life is evident at every turn. Whether you're gazing at raked gravel in a Zen temple courtyard or trekking through ancient cedar groves on a misty mountain, these serene sanctuaries speak to a culture that cherishes seasonal change and ecological balance.

In the chapters ahead, we'll transition into exploring **offbeat cities and towns**, shining a light on pockets of Japan where quirkiness meets tradition—a chance to glimpse how modern creativity intertwines with cultural heritage. Before you leave the tranquility of gardens and wilderness, take a moment to reflect on how these spaces—both crafted and organic—offer a soothing antidote to the rush of modern life. Traveling deeper into Japan's heartland, you'll carry this sense of harmony with you.

Chapter 5: Offbeat Cities & Towns with Quirky Charm

While Tokyo, Osaka, and Kyoto often dominate travelers' itineraries, Japan has no shortage of mid-sized cities and smaller towns that are brimming with personality. These lesser-known locales may not offer the same iconic attractions as the country's megacities, but what they lack in name recognition, they make up for with distinctive cultural quirks, hyper-local festivals, and tight-knit creative communities. In this chapter, we'll delve into the charm of offbeat urban hubs and rural enclaves, revealing how tradition and modernity intersect in surprising ways.

5.1 Why Venture Off the Main Tourist Trail?

1. **Authentic Encounters**

   o **Fewer Crowds, More Conversation**: In smaller communities, shopkeepers and residents often have time to chat, sharing family recipes or neighborhood gossip. Travelers might find themselves invited to impromptu tea gatherings or local celebrations— experiences that rarely happen in high-traffic tourist zones.

- Deep Cultural Immersion: Because these towns are less frequented by outsiders, you'll observe daily rituals and customs in a more unfiltered way. Markets, festivals, and seasonal events unfold with minimal spectacle, allowing visitors to witness genuine local life.

2. **Affordability and Flexibility**

- Lower Living Costs: Hotels and guesthouses in small or mid-sized cities typically charge less than those in Tokyo or Kyoto, freeing up your budget for unique souvenirs, additional travel, or local dining splurges.

- Easy Day Trips: Offbeat towns often serve as gateways to lesser-known hiking trails, hidden hot springs, or scenic drives. Base yourself in a smaller city and explore its surrounding countryside without jostling through tourist bottlenecks.

3. **Surprising Innovation**

- Thriving Startups: Creative entrepreneurs choose smaller cities for lower rents and a relaxed pace. You may stumble upon eco-friendly design studios, artisanal cheese makers, or micro-roasters experimenting with homegrown beans.

○ **Experimental Culture Scenes**: Art collectives, theater troupes, and indie music festivals often thrive in offbeat locales where overhead costs are lower, and the community is eager to embrace new ideas.

Overall, leaving the main tourist track can reward travelers with a richer tapestry of experiences—a chance to see how Japan's traditions persist and evolve in unexpected corners.

5.2 Quirky Urban Centers

Matsumoto (Nagano Prefecture)

- **Castle Town with an Artistic Flair**: Famous for Matsumoto Castle—an imposing black-walled fortress known as the "Crow Castle"—the city also boasts a vibrant contemporary arts scene. Independent galleries dot the downtown streets, showcasing works by regional and international creators.

- **Frog Street (Nawate-dori)**: This whimsical pedestrian lane is adorned with frog statues, frog-themed souvenirs, and snacks like "frog egg" pastries (green tea-flavored treats). The motif stems from local folklore and has become a playful symbol of the city.

- **Music Culture**: Beyond classical concerts, Matsumoto hosts the annual Suwa Lake music festival and jazz performances in cozy bars. You might also encounter street musicians near the castle moat, blending Western brass instruments with traditional Japanese flute.

- **Local Culinary Highlights**: Soba noodles made from locally grown buckwheat, wasabi fresh from nearby Daio Wasabi Farm, and mountain vegetables (sansai) prepared in hearty soups or tempura.

Beppu (Oita Prefecture)

- **Hot Spring Wonderland**: Featuring over 2,000 onsen, Beppu's claim to fame includes eight dramatic geothermal "hells" (jigoku). These range from cobalt-blue acid pools to crimson clay baths, each with atmospheric steam that drifts through narrow lanes.

- **Sand Baths and Mud Pools**: Unique treatments—like being gently buried in naturally heated sand—are said to improve circulation. Meanwhile, thick mud pools with high mineral content attract visitors seeking alternative wellness therapies.

- **Student & Expat Community**: With a sizable international university population, the city has developed a cross-cultural vibe. Food trucks selling fusion street fare and foreign-language film nights coexist alongside traditional ryokan and old-school sento (bathhouses).

- **Nighttime Strolls**: Stepping out after dark, you'll see glowing steam rising from bathhouse chimneys, creating an otherworldly view reminiscent of a retro-futuristic movie set.

Otaru (Hokkaido)

- **Canal-Side Charm**: Otaru's historic warehouses are repurposed as trendy restaurants, microbreweries, and boutiques. Gas lamp-style streetlights reflect off the water at night, making the canal walk especially picturesque.

- **Glass and Music Box Mecca**: The city's glass-blowing tradition emerged from its early days as a trade hub. Today, visitors can craft their own glass trinkets or watch artisans blow molten glass into vases. Otaru's Music Box Museum houses thousands of intricately

73

designed boxes, some featuring local folk tunes.

- **Seasonal Allure**: Beyond the famed Snow Light Path festival in winter, summer offers lush flower gardens, and autumn sees the surrounding hills ablaze in red and gold. Each season transforms Otaru's pastel-hued cityscape into a distinct palette.

- **Seafood Delights**: Being near prime fishing grounds, the city's sushi bars and fish markets brim with fresh catches—squid, scallops, sea urchin, and more.

5.3 Lesser-Known Towns with Surprising Twists

Taketa (Oita Prefecture)

- **A Castle in Ruins**: Perched atop a plateau, Oka Castle's vestiges exude an eerie beauty. Early morning fog often drapes the stone walls, inspiring local legends about ancestral spirits.

- **Showa-Era Nostalgia**: Wandering the old shopping arcades feels like stepping into 1950s Japan. Some shopkeepers still handwrite receipts; antique soda machines dispense retro beverages.

- **Bamboo Lantern Festival**: Each autumn, artisans carve elaborate designs into bamboo stalks, illuminating the streets with flickering candlelight. Musicians, traditional dancers, and street performers elevate the event into a multisensory spectacle.

- **Local Crafts**: Taketa's rural surroundings foster a community of potters, weavers, and dye-makers. Studios frequently offer workshops where visitors can try their hand at shaping clay or natural indigo dyeing.

Onomichi (Hiroshima Prefecture)

- **Temple-Lined Slopes**: Narrow alleys weave uphill past stone walls, hidden shrines, and cat-themed signage (the city is known for its sizable stray cat population). Temple bells punctuate the tranquil atmosphere, blending with the occasional boat horn from the harbor.

- **Literary Legacy**: Renowned Japanese writers like Fumiko Hayashi found inspiration in Onomichi's maritime vistas. A self-guided "literary path" connects passages from their works to real-life locations.

- **Cycle Hub**: As the gateway to the Shimanami Kaidō, Onomichi caters to cyclists with well-maintained rental shops, bicycle-friendly cafes, and scenic rest stops overlooking the

Seto Inland Sea. A handful of local inns even provide post-ride foot baths.

- **Family-Owned Eateries**: From old-school coffee shops serving thick toast slathered in jam to udon joints run by multi-generational families, the culinary offerings reflect the city's slow, steady rhythm.

Kanazawa (Ishikawa Prefecture)

- **Geisha & Samurai Districts**: The preserved architecture in Higashi Chaya (geisha) and Nagamachi (samurai) districts often feels like stepping into Edo-period Japan. In the evening, the echo of shamisen practice might drift through wooden lattice screens.

- **Gold Leaf Craft**: Sample gold-leaf soft-serve ice cream or pick up hand-gilded chopsticks as souvenirs. Workshops explain how local artisans painstakingly hammer gold into ultra-thin sheets.

- **21st Century Museum of Contemporary Art**: Showcasing interactive art installations, the museum's playful vibe contrasts with Kanazawa's historical setting. Exhibits often involve illusions or immersive environments that challenge your sense of space.

- **Culinary Gems**: Kanazawa is famed for kaisen-don (seafood rice bowls), sweet shrimp, and seasonal vegetables from the nearby Kaga region.

5.4 Quirk-Driven Tourism & Local Pride

1. **Mascot Obsession**

   o **Yuru-chara Competitions**: Some towns host events to crown the "cutest" or "most creative" mascot, drawing enthusiasts from across the country. The resulting parades are a riot of cartoonish costumes.

   o **Merchandise Mania**: Mascot-themed keychains, snacks, and apparel line store shelves—purchasing them supports local economies, especially in rural areas that rely on tourism boosts.

2. **Themed Cafés & Museums**

   o **Animal Legends**: A city with a fox folklore might open a fox-themed cafe, while another region with a mythical kappa creature could feature a museum dedicated to sightings and stories.

   o **Science Meets Myth**: Some museums blend historical records with legends, preserving intangible cultural heritage while entertaining visitors. Expect interactive dioramas, VR experiences, or 3D-printed models.

3. **Creative Street Art**

   o **Revitalizing Shopping Arcades**: Once-abandoned shōtengai (covered shopping streets) can be revived with murals, pop-up stores, and weekend festivals. Street art festivals often invite local youth to collaborate with pro artists.

   o **Installations in Nature**: Along scenic riverbanks or countryside trails, you might stumble upon site-specific sculptures, bridging the gap between urban aesthetics and natural landscapes.

5.5 The Value of Offbeat Festivals

Hyper-Local Celebrations

- **Fire & Water Fêtes**: In mountainous regions, torchlit processions celebrate deities that safeguard villagers from avalanches or floods. Down in coastal hamlets, boat processions and waterborne mikoshi highlight maritime blessings.

- **Agricultural Ceremonies**: Rice-planting festivals in spring, scarecrow festivals in late summer, and communal harvest feasts in autumn honor the land's cyclical bounty. Often overlooked by tourists, these gatherings reflect a community's relationship with the earth.

Engaging with the Community

- **Volunteering & Homestays**

  - **Festival Prep**: Tasks range from setting up bamboo arches to rehearsing taiko drumming routines. Immersing yourself in these events fosters genuine friendships with local families.

  - **Cultural Exchange**: Staying in a homestay during festival season can offer a front-row seat to costume-fitting, dance practice, and recipe-sharing for special holiday dishes.

- **Photography & Social Media**

  - **Amplifying Local Voices**: By sharing your images or videos online (with permission), you might help a small festival gain traction, encouraging more visitors—and in turn, more resources for cultural preservation.

- Hashtag Networking: Some local tourism boards track social media hashtags, occasionally reaching out to travelers for featured content or blog collaborations.

5.6 Practical Tips for Exploring Quirky Cities & Towns

1. **Research Local Blogs & Tourism Boards**

   - **Micro-Influencers**: Follow Japanese social media personalities who travel domestically. Their posts often reveal hidden eateries, family-run shops, and lesser-advertised cultural spots.

   - **Tourist Info Centers**: Smaller towns typically staff multilingual help desks with region-specific pamphlets and recommended itineraries.

2. **Use Regional Rail Passes**

   - **Enabling Wanderlust**: Passes like the JR East Pass or other regional deals allow unlimited rides over a set period—ideal if you're hopping between small stations in search of local gems.

- o **Bus and Ferry Networks**: Don't overlook local buses or water taxis, which might be the only way to reach remote mountain villages or coastal enclaves.

3. **Attend Town Hall Events**

   - o **Community Workshops**: From pottery classes to washi papermaking demonstrations, local cultural centers often list upcoming hands-on sessions.

   - o **Language Exchanges**: If you're learning Japanese, drop by a language meetup for a low-pressure chance to practice—and maybe get travel advice from friendly residents.

4. **Respect Local Routines**

   - o **Early Closures**: Family shops may shut their doors at sunset. Plan your meals and sightseeing accordingly.

   - o **Cash Over Card**: Especially in rural pockets, smaller eateries and souvenir stalls might accept only yen notes or coins.

5. **Language Considerations**

   - o **Pocket Wi-Fi or SIM**: Having Google Translate or a dictionary app accessible on the go can save you from confusion at bus stops or mom-and-pop restaurants.

- ○ **Local Dialects**: Even if your standard Japanese is decent, dialects can be challenging. Embrace the variation—locals often find it endearing when visitors attempt their regional phrases.

5.7 Chapter 5 Summary

From hillside cities dripping with nostalgia to hidden ports brimming with creative energy, Japan's offbeat cities and towns invite you to see a more intimate side of the country. In these enclaves, historical remains mingle with avant-garde art collectives; age-old festivals coexist with forward-thinking community projects. The result is a tapestry of cultural evolution that can only be fully appreciated when you step beyond the well-trodden tourist circuit.

In the upcoming Chapter 6, we transition from exploring quirky destinations to savoring **culinary secrets**—from humble family-run diners to elusive, invitation-only pop-ups. Prepare to feast on Japan's hidden gastronomic treasures and discover how regional flavors add nuance to every bite.

Chapter 6: Culinary Secrets
From Local Bistros to Underground Izakayas

Japan's gastronomic prowess goes well beyond sushi, ramen, and tempura. Every region boasts unique flavor profiles shaped by centuries of cultural exchange, climate variations, and local agricultural practices. In this chapter, we'll roam across the culinary landscape—from unassuming backstreet bistros to underground pop-ups—spotlighting the intimate dining experiences that make Japanese food culture so endlessly fascinating.

6.1 Beyond Sushi & Ramen

Regional Specialties

1. **Hokkaido's Seafood Bounty**

   - **Uni & Ikura**: Sea urchin (uni) and salmon roe (ikura) appear in countless forms, including kaisen-don (seafood bowl) and creamy pastas. Some coastal towns host seasonal uni festivals where you can crack open live urchins on the spot.

   - **Jingisukan**: This lamb barbecue tradition involves grilling marinated meat on a dome-shaped skillet. Paired with onions, peppers, and cabbage, it's a convivial meal often enjoyed in beer gardens or rustic log-cabin restaurants. Don't miss the craft beers that pair beautifully with smoky lamb.

2. **Kyushu's Rich Broths**

   - **Tonkotsu Ramen (Fukuoka)**: Pork bones simmered up to 20 hours yield a silky, umami-laden broth. Local "yatai" (food stalls) often line riverbanks, serving steaming bowls to late-night patrons who gather on small stools under glowing lanterns.

   - **Chicken Nanban (Miyazaki)**: Juicy fried chicken marinated in a sweet-and-sour sauce, then topped with homemade tartar. Restaurants compete fiercely for the title of "best nanban," offering subtle variations in marinade.

   - **Kurobuta Pork (Kagoshima)**: Kagoshima's black pigs produce tender, flavorful pork that stars in shabu-shabu or tonkatsu dishes, reflecting the region's thriving livestock industry.

3. **Shikoku's Udon Culture**

- Sanuki Udon (Kagawa): Renowned for its springy, chewy texture. Fans might plan "udon pilgrimages," sampling multiple shops in a single day. Some even mill their own flour or rely on local wheat to perfect the dough.

- Udon Taxi: In Takamatsu, specially trained taxi drivers double as udon guides, ferrying passengers to hidden noodle joints. They also share the history of each establishment, its signature broth, and recommended toppings.

Culinary Adventures Outside Major Hubs

- **Market-Fresh Menus**: Coastal or rural izakayas often scribble the day's specials in chalk, reflecting that morning's catch or farmers' harvest. Adventurous eaters might try lesser-known fish like flying gurnard or regional vegetables rarely seen in supermarkets.

- **Farm-to-Table Trends**: In mountainous prefectures such as Gifu or Yamanashi, small bistros pride themselves on hyper-local produce—grilling foraged mushrooms, plating locally raised venison, or fermenting pickles using spring water.

6.2 Hidden Izakayas and Nightlife Scenes

The Izakaya Culture

A traditional izakaya is more than a bar; it's a communal gathering place where conversation flows as freely as the drinks. Locals unwind after work, travelers share stories, and chefs whip up small plates meant to be passed around.

1. **Local Recommendations**

   o **Word of Mouth**: Hotel concierges or shop owners can direct you to intimate izakayas with no official signage—sometimes hidden behind sliding wooden doors. Be bold and follow these leads to discover a world of home-cooked dishes and warm hospitality.

   o **Specialty Menus**: Some izakayas focus on yakitori (grilled chicken skewers), while others excel at sashimi or simmered offal. Each spot cultivates its niche, refined over years or decades.

2. **Seasonal Menus**

   o **Oden Variations**: In winter, simmering pots of daikon radish, boiled eggs, and

86

fish cakes perfume the air. Chefs might experiment by adding local specialties—like miso-glazed tofu or mountain yam—to traditional dashi.

- **Summer Refreshers**: Cold tofu topped with grated ginger, shaved bonito flakes, and soy sauce, or lightly grilled eel fillets brushed with sweet soy glaze. Perfect for combating the humidity.

3. **Communication & Etiquette**

- **Sociable Spaces**: Counter seating is prime for striking up conversations with the chef or fellow patrons. Polite curiosity about local customs can lead to free samples or tips for other hidden gems.

- **Nomihōdai**: Some izakayas offer a fixed-rate "all you can drink" menu for a set time period. While it's a popular choice for group parties, pace yourself to avoid cultural faux pas.

Yokocho Alleys

- **Golden Gai (Shinjuku, Tokyo)**

  - **Eclectic Themes**: Bars dedicated to punk rock, literary classics, or 1960s film icons nestle side by side along narrow alleys. Space is tight—sometimes only seating five or six.

- o **Late-Night Revelry**: Post-midnight, the energy peaks. Regulars mingle with curious tourists, forging friendships over shared bottles of whiskey or sake.

- **Harmonica Yokocho (Kichijoji, Tokyo)**

  - o **Retro Ambiance**: Named after its cramped rows resembling a harmonica's reed chambers, this warren includes ramen stalls, craft beer bars, and even a small vendor selling homemade pickles.

  - o **Live Music**: On weekends, a guitarist or accordion player may set up near the entrance, turning the alley into an impromptu performance space.

- **Sakaemachi Yokocho (Nagoya)**

  - o **Regional Delicacies**: Miso katsu (fried pork cutlet with red miso sauce) and tebasaki (peppery chicken wings) highlight Nagoya's robust flavors.

  - o **Casual Vibe**: Perfect for both solo travelers seeking conversation and groups celebrating birthdays, promotions, or simply the joy of being together.

6.3 Family-Run Eateries: Heart of the Neighborhood

Kissaten Culture

- **Retro Cafés**

    o **Time Capsules**: Many kissaten were founded decades ago, with minimal renovations. Expect crocheted tablecloths, vintage posters, and a faint aroma of tobacco from an era when indoor smoking was commonplace.

    o **Signature Drinks**: Beyond black coffee, the menu might feature 'Royal Milk Tea' (steeped with whole milk), hand-drip brew poured through flannel filters, or old-school cream sodas.

- **Community Hubs**

    o **Morning Sets**: A popular custom where a cup of coffee includes a small breakfast—like a thick slice of toast, boiled egg, or salad—for a modest fee.

- Inter-Generational Bonding: Seniors and students alike frequent these spots, bridging age gaps. Don't be surprised if a regular offers local sightseeing advice.

Kappo & Shokudō

- **Kappo**: A halfway point between casual izakaya and formal kaiseki, kappo restaurants celebrate the chef's craft. Diners witness each stage of food preparation—filleting fish, plating sashimi, stirring simmering broths—while learning about seasonal ingredients.

- **Shokudō**: These unpretentious diners serve staple dishes—grilled fish, curry rice, donburi (rice bowls)—in hearty portions. Expect plastic display food in the window, neon signs, and friendly banter with the proprietors.

Rural Gems

- **Minshuku Meals**

  - **Harvest-to-Table**: Families running a minshuku often produce their own miso, pickles, or rice. Dinner might feature locally hunted game like wild boar, prepared in a hearty nabe (hot pot).

- o **Seasonal Delights**: In spring, fresh bamboo shoots. Summer: sweet corn and vine-ripened tomatoes. Autumn: chestnuts, persimmons, and matsutake mushrooms. Winter: mountain yams and warming hot pot stews.

- **Community-Driven**: Eating at these establishments means more than a meal—it's a window into how rural communities adapt old recipes for modern palates, often revitalizing diminishing culinary traditions.

6.4 Underground Dining & Secret Pop-Ups

1. **Nomadic Chefs**

   - o **Cross-Cultural Fusion**: A visiting Italian chef might pair local seafood with homemade pasta, or a Peruvian-Japanese duo could spotlight Nikkei dishes using Shimane-sourced ingredients.

   - o **Intimate Gatherings**: Usually limited to a dozen guests, these pop-ups encourage mingling. Diners may leave with new friends or even a tip on another clandestine eatery.

2. **Hidden Themed Restaurants**

   o **Secret Knock or Password**: Entering might require calling a phone number posted on a back alley door or responding to a cryptic Instagram clue.

   o **Immersive Decor**: Interiors could be modeled after a 1920s speakeasy, a retro gaming arcade, or a whimsical forest. Menus might rotate monthly, matching the theme's storyline.

3. **Rooftop Farms**

   o **Urban Farming Collaborations**: Chefs scissor fresh herbs or lettuce leaves moments before plating. Some rooftop venues open to the public on weekends for workshops on composting or vertical gardening.

   o **Twilight Dinners**: Enjoying a multi-course meal while city lights twinkle below and farmland thrives above fosters a unique sense of harmony between nature and urban sprawl.

6.5 Sake, Shochu & Craft Beer
Appreciating Nihonshu (Sake)

- **Terroir Matters**: Sake's flavor hinges on water quality, rice strain, and local yeast varieties. Regions like Niigata, with its pure snowmelt water, produce crisp, dry sake. Meanwhile, Fushimi in Kyoto is known for smoother, softer notes.

- **Visiting Breweries**

  - **Seasonal Sight**: In winter, the aroma of steamed rice drifts from brewhouse vents, mixing with cold mountain air. Many breweries exhibit wooden sugitama (cedar balls) hung at entrances, signaling fresh sake is ready.

  - **Sampling Culture**: Tasting rooms might offer flights highlighting different polishing rates (junmai, ginjō, daiginjō) or unpasteurized nama variants.

- **Sake Bars**

  - **Expert Guidance**: Some bartenders hold sake sommelier certifications, guiding novices to the right label. They may also suggest pairing sashimi, cheese, or even chocolate to accentuate certain flavors.

Shochu's Rise

- **Kyushu Stronghold**

  - **Sweet Potato vs. Barley**: Imo shōchū (sweet potato) can have a robust, earthy aroma, while mugi shōchū (barley) offers a cleaner finish. Kokuto (brown sugar) shōchū from Amami Ōshima adds a hint of caramel sweetness.

  - **Local Pride**: Distilleries often stand at the heart of small towns, hosting tasting events where families gather to celebrate new batches.

- **Cocktail Culture**

  - **Chuhai & Sours**: Shochu mixed with flavored soda or fresh fruit juice is a staple in many izakayas. Grapefruit sours are especially popular, with bartenders squeezing half a grapefruit into a tall glass.

  - **Experimentation**: Younger distillers are infusing shōchū with yuzu zest, green tea, or even coffee, bridging tradition and innovation.

Craft Beer & Beyond

- **Microbreweries**

- o **Regional Ingredients**: Brewers incorporate local produce like yuzu, sansho pepper, or sweet potatoes to craft beers reflecting the region's agricultural identity.

- o **Taproom Culture**: Taprooms in cities like Yokohama, Sapporo, or Nagano often double as community spaces, hosting trivia nights, live music, or beer education events.

- **Beer Gardens**

  - o **Seasonal Outdoor Fun**: Summer beer gardens pop up on department store rooftops or in castle parks. Paired with charcoal-grilled meats and ice-cold mugs, they're a staple of warm-weather socializing.

6.6 Practical Tips for Culinary Explorations

1. **Respect Local Etiquette**

   - o **Slurping Norms**: Enthusiastic slurping for noodles is encouraged, but do it gracefully—excessive noise can appear comedic rather than polite.

- Sharing Plates: Japanese dishes are designed for communal enjoyment. Use the opposite end of your chopsticks when picking from shared plates if no serving utensil is provided.

- Chopsticks Protocol: Refrain from pointing chopsticks at others or passing food from chopstick to chopstick, both considered breaches of dining etiquette.

2. **Reservations and Seating Charges**

- Tabelog & Gurunavi: Check reviews, note that certain highly rated restaurants might not have English-speaking staff. A polite phrase or two in Japanese can go a long way.

- Otoshi (Appetizer Charge): Understand that a small charge for an automatically served appetizer is standard in izakayas—this is not an attempt to upsell.

3. **Dietary Considerations**

- Vegetarian/Vegan: Shōjin ryōri in temple lodgings exemplifies meatless cuisine, but fish-based dashi might creep into everyday restaurant soups. When in doubt, confirm with staff:

"Dashi wa sakana desu ka?" (Is the soup stock fish-based?).

- o **Allergies**: Wheat, soy, and shellfish are common in Japanese cuisine. Carry an allergy card in Japanese to safely communicate your restrictions.

4. **Follow the Season**

- o **Menus in Flux**: Keep an open mind—some items might sell out early, while unexpected specialties could appear based on a fisherman's haul or a farmer's harvest.

- o **Lunchtime Deals**: Many upscale restaurants offer economical lunch sets. Seize this chance to taste haute cuisine without the dinner price tag.

5. **Engage with Locals**

- o **Counter Seating**: Observing the chef's technique—forming nigiri, plating sashimi, or fanning charcoal grills—deepens your appreciation of the culinary craft.

- o **Language Tools**: Knowing phrases like "Omakase de onegai shimasu" (I'll leave it up to the chef) can open doors to unique, personalized meals.

6.7 Chapter 6 Summary

From Hokkaido's briny sea urchin bowls to Kyushu's robust tonkotsu ramen, Japan's regional flavors run the gamut of textures, aromas, and even cooking philosophies. Beneath the bright signs of chain restaurants lie countless hidden bistros, family-run diners, and after-dark pop-ups waiting to share their culinary secrets. Embracing the local seasons, forging connections at intimate counters, and venturing beyond the predictable gastronomic staples will reveal a side of Japanese food culture that speaks to the heart of tradition and innovation.

In the next chapter, we'll pivot from the dinner table to Japan's awe-inspiring landscapes, spotlighting **captivating vistas for every season**—including volcanic terrains, mist-shrouded valleys, and floral extravaganzas where nature takes center stage. Lace up your boots and prepare to explore the lush tapestry of Japan's great outdoors.

Conclusion

Traveling across Japan's hidden gems isn't just a matter of following maps, checking off must-see spots, or gathering the perfect Instagram photos. Rather, it is about allowing yourself to enter into a dialogue with a culture known for its subtlety, gentleness, and capacity to surprise. Along this journey, a pattern emerges: the humblest corners of the country—tiny coastal villages, remote mountain paths, family-run cafés in unassuming towns—offer some of the most profound and memorable experiences.

In a land where centuries-old shrines coexist with avant-garde architecture, and where meticulously preserved customs harmonize with cutting-edge technology, the best discoveries often occur in moments of chance or curiosity. Maybe it's the retired fisherman inviting you into his workshop to see handcrafted fishing nets, or the produce vendor who shares the season's best fruits along with local folklore about river spirits. Through these countless encounters, you piece together an image of Japan that is far richer and more nuanced than any single guidebook could describe.

Understanding the Layers of a Culture

Modern Japan is layered with influences—ancient animist beliefs woven into Shinto traditions, Buddhist rituals from the continent, and a contemporary global outlook that embraces pop culture, tech innovation, and international fusion cuisines. When you step off the bullet train and into a modest station on the outskirts of a lesser-known prefecture, you begin to experience how these layers manifest in everyday life.

One might see an elderly shopkeeper placing fresh flowers at a local shrine before opening up her store, or a group of uniformed students practicing a centuries-old tea ceremony after school. This duality—simultaneous devotion to the past and enthusiasm for the future—anchors Japan's cultural identity in a perpetual balancing act. Understanding these layers doesn't happen in a single trip or with a few pages of reading, but every moment spent in hidden locales deepens your appreciation for these interlocking worlds.

Growth Through Authentic Encounters

At the heart of these travels is the chance for **authentic encounters**—the kind that don't happen on a fast-paced group tour, but arise naturally when you linger in a quiet café or strike up conversation with a local artisan. Each conversation offers a window into regional identity, shaped by weather patterns, local produce, historical events, and personal memories. Through these warm, spontaneous exchanges, you quickly realize that Japan's real allure emerges when you slow down and let the environment guide you.

The True Meaning of Seasonal Living

One of the most striking aspects of Japanese culture is the deep respect for the seasons—a thread woven through every chapter of this book, from the festivals that brighten spring to the cozy hearths that enliven winter. Each month unveils new produce, changing landscapes, and fresh reasons for celebration. Even the simplest meal—like a bowl of miso soup loaded with just-harvested vegetables—can feel like a tribute to nature's timeline.

When you wander off to lesser-known hanami (flower-viewing) spots in a mountain village, or witness a small orchard's harvest festival celebrating freshly picked persimmons, you begin to see how seasonality is more than a quaint custom. It's an ethos that encourages living in tune with the environment, cultivating gratitude for fleeting beauty, and nurturing a sense of community built around anticipating and rejoicing in each seasonal shift. In these quieter locales, you'll often find that residents don't just observe the seasons—they actively celebrate them, weaving them into the region's identity, economy, and social calendar.

The Power of Community Connections

In busier cities, anonymity can cloak daily interactions. But in rural hamlets or small urban enclaves, personal connections often shape the rhythm of life. A shopkeeper might address customers by first name, or a local festival might require the entire town's involvement to set up lanterns or rehearse a communal dance. These bonds aren't simply nostalgic relics—they show how cultural heritage and collective effort can keep local traditions vibrant.

For travelers, being welcomed into these networks is a privilege and an education. A potter in a mountain town might guide you through the tactile joy of shaping clay, discussing how the local river's minerals influence the glaze's color. A fisherman might reveal secret coves where he once saw rare sea life, cautioning you to tread gently to preserve the delicate ecosystem. Each anecdote or lesson underscores that these hidden destinations thrive on cooperation and mutual respect, both among residents and with nature. Participating in that dynamic, even briefly, fosters a sense of belonging and responsibility.

Local Economics and Responsible Tourism

Opting for a night in a small ryokan, purchasing a locally made craft, or visiting a neighborhood eatery run by the same family for generations isn't just about personal enjoyment—it actively contributes to the well-being of the community. Tourism, when done responsibly, supports small businesses and local artisans, encouraging them to preserve traditional techniques that might otherwise vanish under economic pressures. Your presence can be a form of cultural exchange, an opportunity for both visitors and residents to learn from one another.

Embracing Diversity Within Japan

Though it's often portrayed as a cohesive society, Japan is incredibly diverse, spanning subarctic climates in Hokkaido to subtropical islands in Okinawa. Each region offers variations in dialect, cuisine, festivals, and even architecture. By stepping away from the typical route—Tokyo, Kyoto, Hiroshima—you begin to see just how multifaceted the nation is. A single prefecture can contain multiple micro-cultures, from highland farmers to coastal fishers, each with its own history of adaptation to local landscapes.

This diversity also extends to modern subcultures—from anime collectors in rural Tottori to avant-garde theater troupes in smaller Kansai cities. Even local fashion movements can differ dramatically between prefectures. When you travel beyond the usual stops, you expose yourself to an endless kaleidoscope of styles, worldviews, and histories, showcasing that "Japanese culture" is an umbrella term for countless interwoven narratives.

Keys to a Memorable Journey

1. Stay Open to Serendipity

Sometimes the best experiences aren't planned. You might stumble upon a secluded hiking trail while biking to a lesser-known hot spring, or discover an unadvertised festival in the next town over. Allowing space for improvisation in your itinerary fosters a deeper, more organic engagement with your surroundings.

2. Ask Questions, Show Interest

Curiosity is a universal icebreaker. If you see something unusual—a local dish you've never encountered, a shrine with unfamiliar symbols— politely inquire. Most locals, proud of their heritage, will be delighted to share insights, and you may end up with an insider tip or personal anecdote.

3. Learn (and Use) a Few Key Phrases

Even if your Japanese vocabulary is limited, greeting someone with "Konnichiwa" or "Arigatō gozaimasu" can transform a simple transaction into a genuine connection. Attempting local dialect words is often seen as a touching gesture, bridging cultural gaps more effectively than you might imagine.

4. Tread Lightly

Many hidden gems flourish in fragile ecosystems or rely on delicate community balances. Respect local rules about photography, foot traffic, or resource usage. Avoid littering and be mindful not to disturb wildlife. A responsible traveler leaves minimal impact and maximum goodwill.

5. Reflect and Share

Travel's deepest value often emerges afterward—when you share experiences with friends, journal about unexpected discoveries, or incorporate lessons learned into daily life. These reflections keep journeys alive in your memory and can inspire others to seek out their own hidden paths.

A Final Word on Japanese Hospitality

Many visitors remark on Japan's sense of hospitality, or **omotenashi**. In hidden hamlets, this can manifest as a local family inviting you for tea, a station attendant going out of their way to help you catch a rare train connection, or a ryokan owner patiently explaining every dish in your elaborate dinner. Omotenashi is about anticipating needs and ensuring comfort without expecting anything in return, which fosters a sense of profound welcome.

However, it's important to remember that hospitality is a two-way street. Respect the customs of the place you visit, show gratitude for the kindness extended to you, and you'll deepen the mutual appreciation that underpins these encounters. This delicate interplay of hospitality and respect is part of what makes traveling through less-touristed regions so rewarding.

Key Takeaways

1. **Seasonal Awareness**: Japan's seasons shape not only the landscape but also local festivals, markets, and everyday menus. Embrace these changes to appreciate the country in its full cyclical beauty.

2. **Community Immersion**: Treasured moments often arise from spontaneous human connections—someone's story of their grandparents, a handmade craft discovered in a small gallery, or an invitation to join in a local ceremony.

3. **Cultural Etiquette**: Polite gestures and basic Japanese phrases can open a world of deeper respect and understanding. Don't overlook small cultural norms like removing shoes indoors or refraining from eating on the go in rural areas.

4. **Savoring Every Bite**: Regional dishes are living traditions. From mountain vegetables to coastal sashimi, each ingredient ties into a broader story of land, climate, and heritage.

5. **Respect for Nature & Heritage**: Japan's off-the-beaten-track marvels survive thanks to communities that steward them carefully. Your role as a visitor is to support that stewardship—through mindful travel, thoughtful spending, and a reverence for local traditions.

Moving Beyond the Pages

The chapters in this book are only a beginning, an invitation into corners of Japan often overlooked by streamlined travel itineraries. Yet countless surprises still await discovery—abandoned rail lines converted into scenic walking paths, farmer's cooperatives reviving ancient rice varieties, or quiet coastal shrines perched on cliffs battered by winter storms. The more you explore, the more you realize that true wonder lies in the synergy between place and people.

An Invitation to Return

No traveler sees all of Japan in one go. Even multiple journeys can leave you feeling like there's more to uncover—another festival, another gastronomic secret, another breathtaking vantage point. Treat each departure not as a farewell, but as a "mata ne"—a "see you again." Because whether you come back next month, next year, or next decade, Japan's hidden gems and timeless traditions will keep offering new perspectives.

Fostering Long-Lasting Bonds

For many, forging friendships with local hosts, artisans, or fellow travelers is the true highlight of their adventure. These connections often outlast the trip itself, prompting letter exchanges, social media friendships, or plans to reunite. In that sense, exploring lesser-known destinations isn't just about satisfying wanderlust—it's about building a network of global community anchored by mutual curiosity.

Final Thoughts

Japan's unassuming corners hold a magnetic charm: pockets of coastline where families have harvested seaweed for centuries, mountain towns where festivals honoring harvest gods continue unabated, and modern creative enclaves where tradition merge

Made in the USA
Columbia, SC
04 April 2025

56159551R00061